ハワイ島
宙の音
~星空ガイド物語~

A STAR GUIDE'S TALE, Island of Hawai'i

A GIFT FROM THE COSMOS

はじめに
In the Beginning

01 星空との出会い
Meeting the starry sky

02 星空ガイドになりたい！
I wanna be a star guide!

03 ハワイ島の大自然
Nature in Hawai'i

04 ホットスポットの真上にあるハワイ島
Hawai'i, the island above the hot spot

05 自然との繋がりを絶やさないこの島の住民たち
Hawai'i Island residents, truly in touch with nature

06 僕らは宇宙から生まれた
We were born from the Cosmos

07 宇宙も星も人類も、全てがぐるぐる回っている
The Cosmos, the stars, mankind, everything is spinning

08 お役目
A calling

09 宙の音
A gift from the Cosmos

The Beginning

The moment I stepped off the plane my first though was,

"I'm going to be here for the rest of my life."

I still remember how it felt,

like electricity was coursing through my entire body.

Looking back on that feeling now,

I honestly believe it was my body resonating

with the enormous energy of this place.

Fast forward 30 years and I've introduced more than 250,000 people

to the starry sky from that sacred mountain, Mauna Kea.

Even after going to the same place so many times over so many years,

the view takes my breath away to this day.

Stargazing from the slopes of Mauna Kea with so many people over

the years has truly been a gift.

I'm thankful for being able to share that experience with everyone.

はじめに

『死ぬまで僕はここにいるんだ。』飛行機のタラップから降りてきて地面に足が着いた瞬間、全身に電気が走るような感覚をはっきりと覚えています。今思えばこの土地の持つ、とてつもないエネルギーに僕の体が共鳴したからだったと思います。それから35年、述べ25万人以上の方々にマウナケアという聖なる山の頂から見える星空を紹介してきました。こんなに長い間、同じ場所に行っていますが今でも、そこから見える景色に日々感動しています。本当にたくさんの人たちと一緒にこのハワイ島という島で、そしてマウナケアという山の天辺から（この地球という星の上から）星空（宇宙）を眺め、たくさんの感動を共にしてきました。

01

"I need to live on Hawai'i island."
On that desire alone I got a job for a year
and followed my heart to Hawai'i. A year later, with the contract ended,
I was unemployed.
I'm a great lover of fishing so I spent my free time
angling while looking for work as a guide. Unfortunately,
with so few tourists to Hawai'i Island at that time,
there were no opportunities.
My only income was fishing but somehow I managed not to starve.
I sold the fish I caught, traded them for vegetables,
and even sent pictures and wrote articles for monthly fishing magazines.
Looking back on that time now,
I was carefree to the point of being reckless,
but it was such a simple and fulfilling time in my life.

ハワイ島で暮らしたい。その想いだけで1年契約の仕事を見つけ、念願のハワイ島に移住しました。1年後、契約通り無職になった僕は、大好きな釣りに関わる仕事で食べていこうと思い、毎日ガイドの下調べと称して釣りに出かけていました。しかし、まだまだ、観光客の少なかった当時のハワイ島では、釣りのガイドとしての収入はゼロ。収入源は釣った魚を売ったり、野菜と交換したり、時には釣り月刊誌に記事や写真を送ったりして、なんとか食いつないでいました。今思えば、ずいぶんと呑気なもので、少し無謀だったのかもしれませんが、そんな気ままな日々は、とてもシンプルで、一番楽しかった時期だったように思います。

One day a friend of mine from Japan visited the island so I decided to showed him around.

As a photographer he was overwhelmed with all the beauty to capture

and with all the pictures we were taking we stayed out much later than intended.

The sun had set but we were still snapping away.

Saddle Road connects Hilo and Kona

but is so high up that it is frequently inside of the clouds.

At times it can get to the point where you can't see more than a few feet in front of you.

With trepidation in our hearts we set out for our return trip home.

The initial drive was as expected, creeping through a narrow tunnel of

light created by our head lights, but as we approached the entrance to Mauna Kea

at around 6,000 feet, the clouds parted. As relief washed over me,

I glanced up to see the stars as I had never seen them before.

It was a breathtaking sky full of glittering diamonds and a great swathe of the Milky Way.

I was stunned silent by the beauty.

そんなある日、日本から友人がこの島に訪れ、僕は彼をつれて車で島を案内していました。写真家であった友人はこの島の自然に魅せられ至る所でシャッターチャンスを狙っていたので、予定の時刻をはるかに超えて陽が暮れてしまいました。帰り道のヒロからコナに戻るサドルロードは真っ白な霧に包まれ1メートル先も見えない状態でした。僕はヘッドライトの光で出来た白いトンネルを緊張しながら、ただひたすらハンドルを握っていました。すると標高2000メートル地点のマウナケアの入り口付近に通りかかった時に、一気に霧が晴れてきました。ほっと胸を撫でおろした瞬間、僕の目の前に今までに見たこともない景色が現れたのです。満天の星空。その中に堂々と横たわる天の川。すげー。こんな星空みたことない。。。

サドルロード
Saddle Road

Mauna Kea
← Access Road

サドルロードから見える星空
The starry sky from Saddle Road

From that day on I couldn't get those stars out of my head.
I wanted to see what
they looked like from the summit of Mauna Kea.
Before I knew it I was in my truck slowly
making my way up the mountain around sunset time.
What greeted me at the summit was
a setting sun and a rich sky full of vibrant colors.

翌日から僕の頭の中は
あの星空でいっぱいになってしまいました。
マウナケア山頂に行ってあの星空を見てみたい。
気付けば僕はハンドルを握りあの夜、霧が晴れた場所
サドルロードからマウナケア向かう坂道を
ドキドキしながら山頂に向かっていました。
ちょうどサンセットの時間。
僕を出迎えたのは、今まで見たことのない
美しい色をした空に沈みゆく太陽でした。

マウナケア山頂
The summit of Mauna Kea

標高4205メートルのマウナケア山頂からの夕陽
Sunset from the summit of Mauna Kea, 4,205 meters above sea-level (13,803 feet)

After the Sun set

it truly felt like I was gazing into space.

I could feel the turning of the earth.

太陽が沈んだ後は、
まさにそこは宇宙の景色。
地球が回っているのを
実感しました。

I could hardly contain myself.

I thought to myself,

"Everyone else needs to see this,

to experience this."

マウナケア山頂付近のサンセットが終わり星空に変わるとき
The transition from sunset to the night sky.

『嗚呼。この感動を伝えたい。』

みんなに、見せなきゃ!!

02

I began thinking of how I could show others the beauty in the night sky
that had charmed me so thoroughly.
I wanted to make it my career so I set about
turning that wish into reality.
In the beginning there were some hurdles,
most notably that I didn't speak English
and I had no idea how to start a company.
It took me two and a half years to get everything in order
and get permission to create and run a star gazing tour company.
During that time I learned something very important
about the mountain, Mauna Kea.

マウナケア山頂での見たこともない星空の魅力にとりつかれた僕は、どうにかしてこの景色を多くの人に見せることはできないかを考え始めました。そのためにはツアー会社を設立する必要があることがわかりました。英語も喋れない、会社を作る手続きも全くわからない。そんな僕が、星空をガイドするための営業許可を取得するのには、2年半の歳月が必要でした。しかし、その時間の中で僕は、マウナケアという山についての大切なことを理解していきました。

On this mountain,
in the area classified as a science reserve,
there are observatories belonging to countries all over the world.
There are insects and plants that don't exist anywhere else.
There are sacred sites,
and indeed the entire mountain is sacred,
belonging to the native Hawaiian people.

この山は、世界各国から集まった天文台が数多く
あり『サイエンスリザーブ』としてハワイ州の
管轄下にあるエリアで、山頂近くに生息する昆虫
や植物は地球上でもここにしか生息しないため
自然保護区にも指定されているため営業許可を
とるのが困難なエリアであること。そしてこの
山は、この島々の先住民であるハワイアンの人
たちにとって、一番の聖地であったこと。

ワイコロアから見えるマウナケア
Mauna Kea from Waikoloa

In Hawai'i there is a creation story known as Kumulipo.

It is a legend that begins with the creation of the Hawaiian islands

by the male god of the sky, Wakea,

and the female god of the earth, Papa.

Mauna Kea is , according to the legend, where the two gods met.

Therefore, Mauna Kea is sacred to all the native tribes of Hawai'i.

With this in mind I began to understand the energy that

I felt when stargazing from it's slopes

and to realize it's power and significance.

ハワイには、クムリポと言う創世物語（日本で言えば、日本書紀）があります。その中にハワイの島々は、天空の男神・「ヴァケア」と大地の女神『パパハナウモク』から生まれたと言う一節が有る伝説です。その伝説のなかでヴァケアとパパが出会う場所が、なんとこのマウナケアの山頂だったのです。マウナケアはすべての部族のハワイアンにとって聖地だったのです。それを知り、マウナケアで見た星空がなんであんなエネルギーに満ちていたのかを理解することが出来ました。それからというもの、僕のマウナケアに対する想いはどんどんと深まっていきました。

キラウエア火山の噴煙と天の川
A billowing eruption from Kilauea volcano frames the Milky Way.

そして1992年。僕は、小さな7人乗りのバンを手に入れ、星空ガイドとして営業を始めることが出来ました。

Then, in 1992, I obtained a 7 passenger van and began working as a stargazing guide.

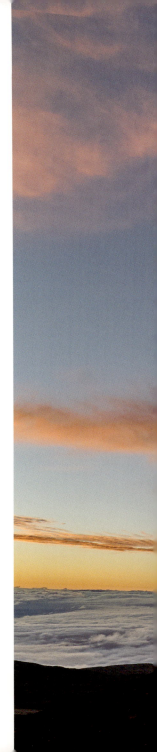

マウナケア山頂
The summit of Mauna Kea

03

I have been truly blessed to be able to spend more than half of my life in this paradise called Hawai'i Island.

Hawai'i Island has 11 of the 13 world climates within it's borders.

The only climates it doesn't have are

what can be found in the Sahara Desert or the North and South Poles.

僕は本当に幸せなことに、人生の半分以上も、この大自然に囲まれたハワイ島という天国のような島で過ごす事が出来ています。日本の四国の半分くらいの大きさのこの島には、地球上にある13の気候区分のうち11の気候帯があります。ないのは、極気候とよばれる南極、北極などの特殊な気候区分と、サハラ気候と呼ばれる砂漠の気候区分だけで、あとの11区分の気候帯が全てこの島には存在しているのです。

ヒロ湾から望むマウナケア
Mauna Kea from Hilo bay

プナルウ黒砂海岸のカメ
Green sea turtles at Punalu'u black sand beach

ワイピオ渓谷のヒイラベの滝
Hi'ilawe falls in Waipi'o valley

ワイピオ渓谷の野生の馬
Wild Horses in Waipi'o valley

パーカー牧場から見たマウナケア
Mauna Kea from Parker ranch

フクロウ、旧サドルロードにて
Owl at the old saddle road

キラウエア溶岩台地に咲くオヒアレフア
Ohia Lehua tree blooming in the lava fields of Kilauea volcano

*Driving around this island you can view
a wealth of different scenery.
You can be driving on a straight road
through jet black lava flows
and suddenly find yourself in a rich green jungle.
Then, looking up, you can see
a perfectly clear azure sky,
a vast grassy mountain side,
and a twinkling white snowy mountaintop.
With such a variety,
it's just like driving around a miniature earth.*

この島を車に乗ってドライブしていると様々な景色に出会うことができます。見渡す限り真っ黒な溶岩をひたすらまっすぐに突き抜ける道、ジャングルのような密林をくぐり抜ける道、真っ青な空を背景に丘の稜線にそって続く緑色の牧草の中をゆっくりとカーブしながら続く道……
まるで、ミニチュアの地球を一周しているようかのような景色のバリエーションを楽しむことができるのです。

マウナケア・アクセスロード
Mauna Kea access road

サウスポイントに続く道
The road to south point

マウナケア・アクセスロード
Mauna Kea access road

Living on this island, with the wealth of nature,

you can understand what nature is to a fine degree.

Nature weaves together

all the natural phenomena; the lives of plants, animals,

and people with the wind, rain, sun, and snow.

Hawai'i island is a place where

you can feel these natural phenomena close around you.

The wind blows, the sun shines, the rain and snow fall.

Occasionally lava flows and volcanoes erupt.

You truly get the feeling that the earth is alive.

豊かな自然のバリエーションを持つこの島に住んでいると
『自然とは何か』を敏感に感じとることができます。自然を
織り成しているのは植物、動物、人間などの生命。そして風、
雨、雪などの地球が動いていることで産まれる現象です。
風が吹いたり、雨が降ったり、雪が降ったり、時には火山灰や
溶岩が流れてきたり。そんな現象を真近で感じながら生活して
いると『地球も生きて いるんだ。』と強く実感するのです。

旧サドルロード
Old Saddle Road

04

Off the shore of Hawai'i Island near the Kilauea Volcano is a place
called the hot spot where lava leaks,
filled with energy from within the Earth.
All of the 132 Hawaiian islands were created by
this release of lava from the hot spot.
All of the islands were then transported to their current location
by the movement of the Pacific plate.
The hot spot is active even now,
boiling away underneath the island of Hawai'i.

ハワイ島の南、キラウエア火山の沖合の海底にはホットスポット
と呼ばれる溶岩溜まり（地球の核からのエネルギーが溢れ出
る場所）があります。132 島に及ぶハワイ諸島全ての島々は、
そのホットスポットの噴火活動により出来たものです。それぞれ
の島々が太平洋プレートの移動により現在の場所に移動しました。
今でもそのホットスポットは活発に活動していて、現在その真上
にあるのがハワイ島です。

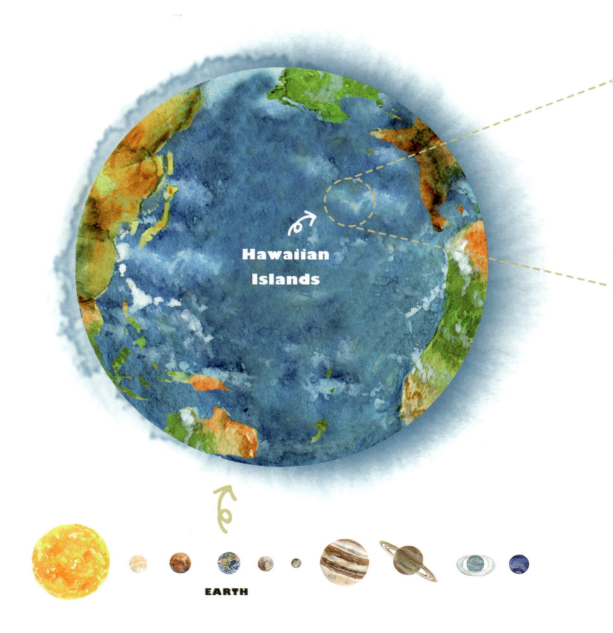

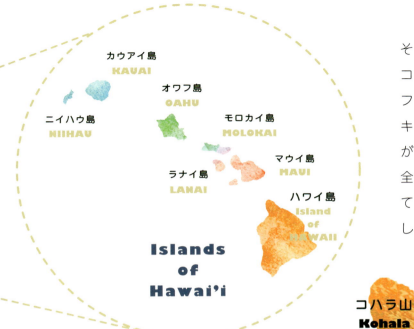

そのホットスポット上にコハラ山、マウナ・ケア、フアラライ、マウナ・ロア、キラウエアの5つの火山が順番に活動してこの島全体が出来ました。そして今でも、この島は成長し続けています。

Above the hot spot there are
5 volcanoes:
Kohala,
Mauna Kea,
Mauna Loa,
Hualalai,
and Kilauea.
They overlap to form
the island of Hawai'i which is,
even now, continuing to grow.

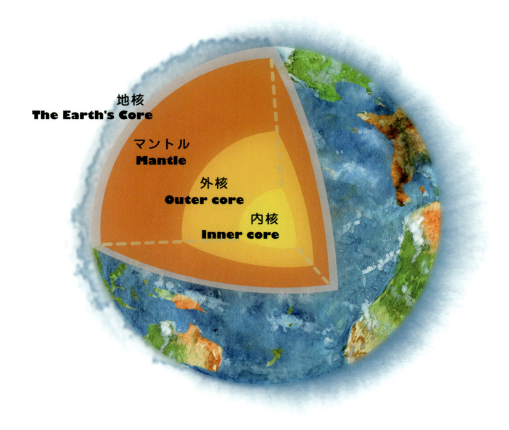

Hot Spots are where magma erupts from the mantle through the crust.
The Hawaiian Islands were born in this way,
millennia upon millennia of lava piling up on the ocean floor,
breaking the surface to form islands,
and then sliding to the north on a tectonic plate.
Each of the islands that make up our Hawai'i,
from Niihau to Maui have gone through this,
with Hawai'i Island above the Hot Spot today.

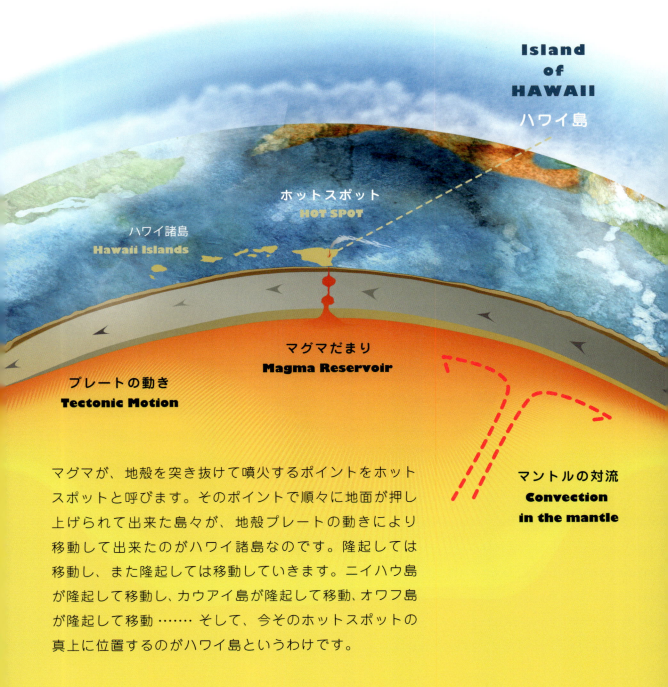

マグマが、地殻を突き抜けて噴火するポイントをホットスポットと呼びます。そのポイントで順々に地面が押し上げられて出来た島々が、地殻プレートの動きにより移動して出来たのがハワイ諸島なのです。隆起しては移動し、また隆起しては移動していきます。ニイハウ島が隆起して移動し、カウアイ島が隆起して移動、オワフ島が隆起して移動……そして、今そのホットスポットの真上に位置するのがハワイ島というわけです。

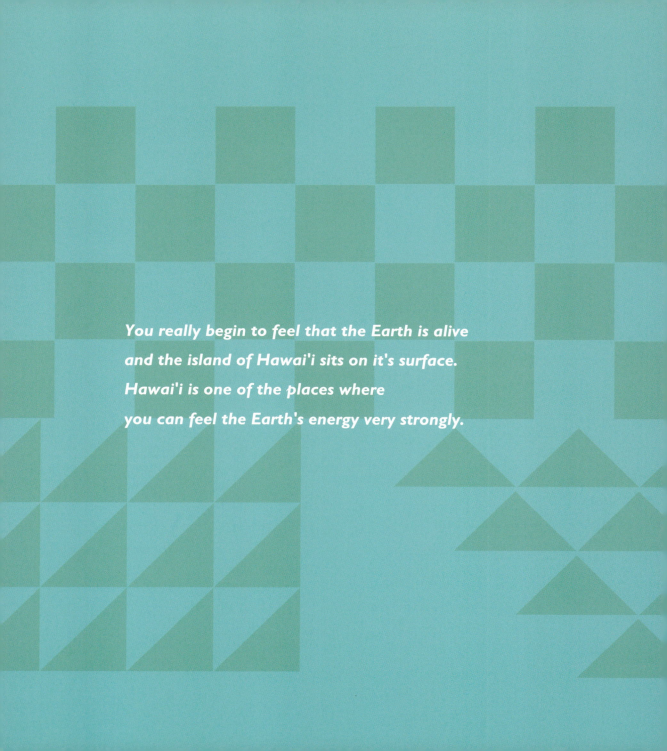

*You really begin to feel that the Earth is alive
and the island of Hawai'i sits on it's surface.
Hawai'i is one of the places where
you can feel the Earth's energy very strongly.*

地球も生命を持った生き物で
あることに気づきますよね。
ハワイ島はその地球という
生き物の表面にあって、
その生命エネルギーをとっても
感じられやすい場所に
位置しているんです。

05

I think Hawai'i island is considered heaven because of the kindness
and serenity of the people living there.
The culture of the ancient Hawaiians remains even now,
their descendants respect and revere nature.
They never forget to be grateful for the natural world.
Much of the recreation in Hawai'i involves nature,
such as Hula, surfing, horseback riding, and fishing.
You can really feel the energy and power from becoming one with nature
and by enjoying nature in a natural setting.
Humanity truly is lucky to have been born on this rock
hurtling through space that we call Earth.

ハワイ島が天国と呼ばれる理由には、そこに住む人たちの優しく穏やかな雰囲気が挙げられると思います。この島の先住民であったハワイアン達の文化が残っているおかげで、この島の人々は自然を敬い、自然への感謝を忘れることはありません。また、フラダンスやサーフィン、ダイビング、釣りなどの自然と融合する遊びも盛んです。自然と一体になることで、人間が元気になるということを実感できるからだと思います。自然の中で、自然と一緒に遊ぶ。これこそが、この大きな宇宙の中で、地球という美しい星に生まれてきた人間の特権なのではないかと思います。

ホノコハウ
Honokohau

プウコホラ・ヘイアウ
puukohola heiau

プウホヌア・オ・ホナウナウ
Pu'uhonua o Honauunan

カロコビーチ
Kaloko Beach

06

From the earliest days, humanity has been gazing at the stars, marveling at their beauty, and pondering their hopes and dreams. People will go on far into the future delighting at the beauty of a sunset, dreaming with the starry sky, and being reinvigorated by the sunrise. Everyone wanting to see a sky full of the most beautiful stars comes to this island.
Standing on Mauna Kea, gazing at the sky you can truly understand why it is considered the gateway to the stars.

太古の昔から、人々は星空を眺め様々な想いを感じ、美しい
自然の景色に癒されてきました。そしてこれからも人々は
夕陽に感動し、星空を眺め想いをはせ、朝陽から希望をもらい
生きていくのだろうと思います。満天の星空を見たいという
方々が次々とこの島に訪れマウナケアという宇宙の入り口
から、果てしない宇宙に思いを馳せている姿をみていると
それを確信できるのです。

マウナケアの山頂に横たわる天の川
The summit of Mauna Kea cradled by the Milky Way

In the vastness of the universe our sun was born,

then the Earth,

and finally humanity.

大きな宇宙の営みの中で、
太陽が生まれ、
地球が生まれ、
その上に、我ら人類が生まれました。

天の川
The Milky Way

*Our life force comes from
and is connected with that of the universe.*

私たちの生命エネルギーは、
その源である宇宙のエネルギーに繋がっています。

郵便はがき

１１２-８７３１

料金受取人払郵便

小石川局承認

1737

差出有効期間
平成30年10月
1日まで
切手をはらずに
お出しください

東京都文京区音羽二丁目十二番二十一号

講談社エディトリアル　行

ご住所	□□□-□□□□			
(フリガナ) お名前			男・女	歳
ご職業	1. 会社員　2. 会社役員　3. 公務員　4. 商工自営　5. 飲食業　6. 農林漁業　7. 教職員 8. 学生　9. 自由業　10. 主婦　11. その他（			）
お買い上げの書店名		市 区 町		書店
今後、講談社より各種ご案内などをお送りしてもよろしいでしょうか。 送付をご承諾いただける方は○をおつけください。				承諾する

TY 000015-1609

愛読者カード

今後の出版企画の参考にいたしたく、ご記入のうえご投函くださいますようお願いいたします。

本のタイトルをお書きください。

a 本書をどこでお知りになりましたか。

　　1．新聞広告（朝、読、毎、日経、産経、他）　　2．書店で実物を見て
　　3．雑誌（雑誌名　　　　　　　　　　　）　　4．人にすすめられて
　　5．書評（媒体名　　　　　　　　　　　）　　6．Web
　　7．その他（　　　　　　　　　　　　　　　　　　　　）

b 本書をご購入いただいた動機をお聞かせください。

c 本書についてのご意見・ご感想をお聞かせください。

d 今後の書籍の出版で、どのような企画をお望みでしょうか。
　興味のあるテーマや著者についてお聞かせください。

ご協力ありがとうございました。

イーターカリーナ星雲
Eta Carinae nebula

ドームが開いたすばる天文台
The Subaru Observatory opened to the stars

子持ち銀河
M51

*Gazing at the stars and pondering
their meaning can even inform our daily lives.*

宇宙を感じることは
あなたの人生においても大きなヒントを
与えてくれるものです。

07

*Humanity has created so much in it's history.
Things such as television, cars, planes,
and the internet are a testament to human creativity and imagination.
However, nothing we create can surpass that made by nature.
This is a foregone conclusion as we are just one part of one star system
in a universe full of countless stars.*

これまで、人間は様々なものを創り出してきました。テレビ、車、飛行機そしてインターネット。その全ては人間の英知を結集したもので素晴らしい発明です。しかし、我々人間が作り出すものは全て人間の英知を誇るものであるものの、自然を超えるものはありません。これは当たり前のことで人間が自然を超えることは出来ないからです。なぜなら我々人間は、この宇宙の中の数え切れないほどある星々の、ひとつの星の中の、ひとつの生命体にすぎないからです。このルールではなく事実は人間がどんなにあがいても変えられることはできません。

太陽系という言葉は、ご存知だと思います。
太陽があって、水星があって、金星があって、地球。
そして 、火星 、木星 、土星……
我々人間が生息する地球という星が属しているのが「太陽系」です。
太陽の周りをぐるぐると回る星たちのひとつのチーム名ですね。
この「太陽系」チームは太陽を中心に、ぐるぐると周りながら
さらには天の川銀河系と呼ばれている渦巻き銀河に属していて
その銀河の中心を太陽と一緒に、ぐるぐると回っているんです。

We have all heard the phrase 'solar system' before.
There's the sun, Mercury, Venus, the earth,
and all the other planets so familiar to us.
Coming from the name of the sun, Sol,
the solar system is the name of the team our little earth belongs to,
everyone revolving around the sun.
As we all revolve around the sun however,
our sun is also part of a much larger group of
stars revolving around the center of the Milky Way galaxy.

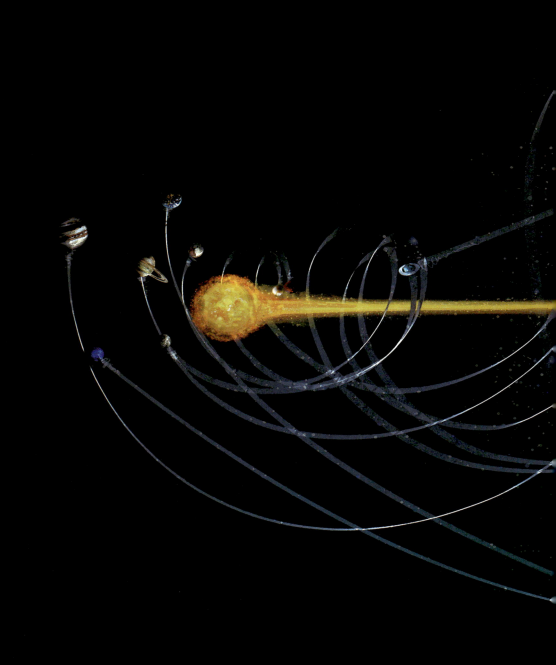

地球の自転で、ぐるぐる。
太陽を回る公転で、ぐるぐる。
そしてまた、天の川銀河を回る回転で、ぐるぐる。
そして、そのまた大きな銀河団に繋がる回転で、ぐるぐる。
そのまた……
ぐるぐる。
ぐるぐる。
ぐるぐる。

ミクロの原子の世界から、マクロの銀河の世界まで、
想像のつかない高速で回転することで宇宙は成り立ち、
調和が保たれ存在しています。

The earth spins, revolves around the sun.

The sun spins, revolves around the center of the Milky Way.

The Milky Way turns...

Spinning, revolving, turning...

From the micro world of the atom to the macro world of galaxies,

the universe consists of things.

spinning around each other unimaginably fast.

This harmony is maintained and existence continues.

日々を過ごしていると、自分たちがこんなに 広い空間
の中にいて、こんなにも大きく、動いていることなん
て実感する機会はほとんど まったくありませんよね。
でも、星空ガイドという職業をしていて、
日々、マウナケアの山頂で星を眺めていると

そのぐるぐるを実感できるんです。

地球って、やっぱり回っているんだなと。

Even though we live and pass our days here,
rarely do we have the chance to recognize the enormity of the space
we live in or feel it's movement.
However, when you work as a stargazing guide on Mauna Kea
and see those stars everyday, you begin to feel it.
Yes, the Earth truly is moving.

マウナケア山頂
The summit of Mauna Kea

しし座流星群、2001年
Leonid meteor shower 2001

マウナロアからみたマウナケア
Mauna Kea from Maunaloa

It's been 25 years since I started showing others the stars.
I've shared this experience, this amazing starry sky,
with so many others from atop this mountain called
Mauna Kea on this island called Hawai'i.
Ever since that moment I first saw the stars from the entrance to Mauna Kea
and thought, "Everyone needs to see this!",
 I felt that star gazing could be my career but
after walking this road for so long I now realize that it wasn't a career,
it was a calling.

星空ガイドを始めてから 25年。本当にたくさんの人たちと一緒にこのハワイ島という島で、そしてマウナケアという山の天辺から（この星の上から）星空（宇宙）を眺め、たくさんの感動を共にしてきました。この綺麗な星空をみんなに見せなきゃ！というあの一瞬の思いから始まった『星空ガイド』は、長い歳月を経て、今では職業という枠を超え、この星に生まれてきた僕の人生の『お役目』なんだということに気がつきました。

マウナケア山頂
The summit of Mauna Kea

5:50 a.m.

マウナケア山頂
The summit of Mauna Kea

6:05 a.m.

マウナケア山頂
The summit of Mauna Kea

12:00 p.m.

マウナケア山頂
The summit of Mauna Kèa

7:05 p.m.

マウナケア山頂

The summit of Mauna Kea

1:00 a.m.

The sun rises then sets.

The moon and the stars come out.

The sun comes back again.

One revolution of the Earth, we call this a day.

It's the easiest way we feel the rhythm of the universe.

Within that rhythm, air, water, people, animals, plants, and bugs,

everything that is on the Earth combines to form the melody of nature.

Whether it's at sunrise or sunset,

it's always worth it to go somewhere that you can see the sky.

It's even fun to just speculate about how the moon will look that night.

By matching the beat of your own existence to the melody

created by nature you can reset your soul back to a tranquil and placid state.

It's easily achievable by anyone.

朝陽が昇り、夕陽が沈み、月や星が現れる。
そしてまた陽がのぼる。
地球が自転によって、ひとまわりするのが1日というリズム。
それが、我々に一番身近な宇宙のリズムです。

そのリズムの中で、
空気や水、そして我々人間や動物、昆虫や植物などの
全ての生命が重なり合い、
『景色』というメロディーを奏でているのです。

朝陽の時間に、夕陽の時間に、空が見えるところに
行くだけでもいいでしょう。
今夜、月が、どんな形をしているのかを
楽しみにするのもいいでしょう。

自然の営みに波長を合わせ、
『景色』というメロディーに
自分自身の『鼓動』を重ねることで

本来、自分が持っている心穏やかで素直な状態に
リセットすることが出来るのです。

そしてそれは、
誰にとっても実に簡単に出来ることなのです。

標高3500M地点で現れた虹
A rainbow at 11,500' elevation

フアラライ沖に沈むスーパームーン
A setting super moon off of Hualalai bay

サウスポイントからの南十字星
The Southern Cross from South Point

ムーンボー（満月の光で夜中にできる虹）
A 'moonbow' (a rainbow made at night with the light of the full moon)

Even though it's the same place,
no matter how many times I see it,
even thousands and thousands of times,
I can appreciate it's beauty.
Every time I go there I think to myself,
"How lucky could I be to be born on this planet
with these beautiful stars all around me."

明けの明星
Venus

同じ場所から見る景色なのに、
何度見ても、美しい。
何千回見ても、美しい。

それを感じる度に、
僕は、この星に生まれてきて本当に幸せ者だな。
って感謝の気持ちでいっぱいになるんです。

マウナケア山頂
The summit of Mauna Kea

これからも
この美しい地球と人間が、
いつまでも仲良く
暮らせていけますように。

May all of humanity and this beautiful earth
forever peacefully coexist.

Afterword

It was in 2010, while on a business trip to Hawai'i Island. I ended up staying at Sunny's place through a series of unusual circumstances. Despite having just met we became fast friends through a mutual love of photography and astronomy. From then on, a few times a year I would find myself flying off to Hawai'i to immerse myself in nature, get an infusion of Mana (energy) from the summit of Mauna Kea, and speak at length with Sunny. I feel so fortunate to have been able to forge such a connection. Everyday life in Tokyo, working endlessly, always having the feel of some looming deadline...those times in Hawai'i, surrounded by nature with Sunny really helped me feel human again. It became a kind of natural rehabilitation therapy. Sometimes in a kayak, sometimes on some lava, and sometimes sitting in the sand on a secret beach, I would absorb Sunny's words, pondering, laughing, and being healed by them. One day I found myself thinking, "It's such a waste to keep this only to myself." Sunny is fond of saying, "You have to realize the things you picture in your mind." I made up my mind, and without even having a publisher in mind we began creating this book. Luckily for us, Sunny had a mountain of nature photography accumulated and I had experience designing dozens of photo books. We also had the shared memories of 7 years of conversations. Creating the book went suspiciously smooth and we had a load of fun doing it. Occasionally in Hawaii, occasionally in Tokyo, and even sometimes in Shonan, we sorted out what we wanted to impart to people in front of a computer screen. After a while I began to get the feeling that we were on to something, that it was all coming together. The next step was to figure out how to get this out into the world. We began by finding a certain person's name on the internet. We then found ourselves benefitting from some unbelievable coincidences and being surrounded by amazing support staff...all leading to me writing this afterword now. I truly feel that our thoughts and our energy, they reach out and form new connections. Now, looking forward, thinking about putting this book into the hands of the people that need it and the energy that will create...I can hardly wait.

Kozo
Fujita

あとがき

2010年、仕事でハワイ島に行った時のことでした。ひょんなきっかけから、僕はサニーさんのご自宅にお世話になることになりました。写真好き、宇宙好きという共通点で、初対面にも関わらず意気投合しました。それからというもの年に数回、ハワイ島の大自然に飛び込みマウナケアの山頂でエネルギーを注入し、サニーさんと大いに語らう。そんな素晴らしいご縁を頂くことができました。東京で休みもなく毎日が締め切りのような日々を過ごしていた僕にとって、大自然の中でサニーさんと過ごす日々は、本来の人間のペースを取り戻すための儀式（自然への定期入院？）のようになっていきました。時にはカヤックの上で、時には溶岩の上で、時には秘密のピーチで全身砂の中に埋まりながら、サニーさんが呟く一つ一つの言葉に頷き、笑い、助けられたものです。そしてある時、思ったのです。これは僕一人のものにしておくのは勿体無い。サニーさんのつぶやきの中に、「頭の中でイメージしたことは必ず現実化する」というのがあります。よし！それではその通りやってみよう！ということで、その時から僕たちは出版元さえも決まっていない、この本を創り始めました。幸いなことに、僕らの元にはサニーさんが撮りためてきた膨大な数の自然の写真、そして僕には、過去何冊もの写真集のデザインをした経験がありました。そして何より7年間、共に語り合った想いがありました。本を創る行程は本当にスムーズで非常に楽しい時間でした。時にハワイ島で、時に東京で、時に湘南で、パソコンの画面を眺めながら、伝えたいことを2人でまとめていきました。そしてようやく、いい感じになったね！と一息ついたところで、僕らは考え始めました。さて、この本をどうやって世の中に出そうか？僕らは、ある人物の名前をインターネットで見つけるところから始めました。そこから繋がっていったご縁は、見事に偶然を超えた必然に代わり、素晴らしいスタッフの方々のご援助を得て、僕は今こうやってこのあとがきを書いています。人の想いもエネルギーのひとつで、そのエネルギーが縁を伝って拡まる。そんなことを実感しています。そしてこの本が、この本を見るべき人の手に渡り、新たなエネルギーが生まれることをイメージすると本当に楽しみでなりません。

2017年10月　湘南にて　藤田恒三

著者紹介

サニー武石

ハワイ島、マウナケア山頂にて星空やサンセット、サンライズを見学する星空ツアーを日本人で初めて行った『元祖星空ガイド』。ツアー会社、太公望ハワイの代表でハワイ島星空ガイドの代表。いままでに25万人以上の日本人を「宇宙の入り口」といわれるマウナケアの山頂へ誘い、大自然の美しさ、宇宙の神秘を伝えている。
www.taikobo.com

藤田恒三

アートディレクター。航空会社の仕事で世界36都市の撮影を敢行中にハワイ島でサニー武石と出会う。それをきっかけに自然の中に身を置くことで得るインスピレーションの大切さに気づく。2012年から拠点を持たずにハワイ島、バリ島のなどの南の島の文化、自然によりそった生活を体験。2017年拠点を日本に戻し活動を再開。企業のブランディング、ビジュアルコミュニケーションに関わる分野で活動中。
www.kozofujita.com

ハワイ島 宙の音
星空ガイド物語

2017年12月15日　第1刷発行

著者　サニー武石　藤田恒三
発行者　鈴木哲
発行所　株式会社　講談社
〒112-8001　東京都文京区音羽2丁目12-21
　　　　（販売）03-5395-3606
　　　　（業務）03-5395-3615

編集　株式会社講談社エディトリアル
　　　代表　堺公江
〒112-0013　東京都文京区音羽1丁目17-18 護国寺SIAビル
　　　　（編集部）03-5319-2171

印刷所　大日本印刷株式会社
製本所　大口製本印刷株式会社
装　丁　藤田恒三

定価はカバーに表示してあります。

本書のコピー、スキャン、デジタル化等の無断複製は著作権法上での例外を除き禁じられています。本書を代行業者等の第三者に依頼してスキャンやデジタル化することはたとえ個人や家庭内の利用でも著作権法違反です。落丁本・乱丁本は購入書店名を明記のうえ、小社業務部あてにお送りください。送料小社負担にてお取替えいたします。なお、この本についてのお問い合わせは、講談社エディトリアルまでお願いします。

©SUNNY TAKEISHI　KOZO FUJITA 2017　Printed in Japan
ISBN 978-4-06-220894-9
NDC595　120p　21cm